A Passion for Holiness:

For those wanting more

Matt Friedeman

Teleios Press

TELEIOS PRESS

http://www.teleiospress.com

As obedient children, do not be conformed to the passions of your former ignorance, but as he who called you is holy, you also be holy in all your conduct, since it is written, "You shall be holy, for I am holy."

1 Peter 1:14-15

Introduction

This booklet can certainly be used individually for personal devotions and inspiration. But it was originally designed to help families and groups in the local church count up the fifty days to Pentecost beginning with Easter Sunday. At Pentecost the Holy Spirit came in a powerful way after the resurrection of Jesus, and the world was thereafter substantially different.

But here is the point. Above all the Holy Spirit came to make people holy. If we forget that vital lesson, we reduce the Spirit's work to the periphery of the Christian life and not see it at the center, where it belongs.

Many local churches do little to celebrate the birthday of the Church. But should we not commemorate this day by remembering how the Holy Spirit filled the believers and thus made them holy, how 3,000 were baptized and how the Church began to march across the Roman Empire and beyond spreading the faith? Additionally, might the Lord also want us to get ready for deeper life in Him today and a harvest of souls in our own local communities?

This little devotional and discussion guide attempts to aid in that preparation for Pentecostal reality. It is designed for married couples, families, friends, small groups or churches to read a daily passage concerning holiness, delve into its meaning and then challenge each other with a discussion question or two. Prayer prompts are provided to help participants cultivate open hearts to live out our call to holiness.

Suggested weekly memory verses are intended to focus the mind on various aspects concerning the holy life. Some churches will choose to reinforce these lessons through sermons and small group Bible studies.

Enjoy your journey deeper into the life our Holy One desires for us. These lessons are by no means a comprehensive guide to holiness, as if there could ever be such a thing. But if you are counting towards Pentecost this guide can help you prepare for your most meaningful and powerful celebration of that day. If you are using this small volume for personal use any other time of the year may God nonetheless richly bless you with His purifying, empowering holy Presence.

Day One

Week One Memory Verse: 1 Peter 1:14-15 (see p. 62)

Today's Verse: "God called to him out of the bush, 'Moses, Moses!' And he said, 'Here I am.' Then he said, 'Do not come near; take your sandals off your feet, for the place on which you are standing is holy ground.'" (Exodus 3:4-5)

In Exodus 3 God chose the word that He would use to best describe Himself: holy/*qadosh*.[i] But there was a problem; the Canaanites had such things as holy prostitutes for their own temple rites. In other words, what was sacred and set aside for the gods was despicable to the one true God. So this is what happened in the book of Exodus: God told Moses to take his shoes off for he was now on holy ground. And what was it that made the ground holy? The presence of God. Only the God of Israel and that which was associated with Him was to be reckoned holy.

In the New Testament, with a different language, word choices concerning God still had to be made. Five terms were available to the writers of the Jesus account: *hieros, hosios, semnos, hagios, hagnos*. Not unlike the Old Testament era, each had negative associations with pagan gods, their temples and repugnant ritual practices. So the Greek word *hagios* was selected as the New Testament equivalent for *qadosh*. *Hagios* appeared least in Greek literature and at the time was used in reference to neither god nor man. Least familiar, least corrupted.

Words and concepts cannot adequately describe God without God filling those terms with His own content. He alone can describe His own nature and what that nature means in the lives of His faithful.

Question: Holiness is the essential nature of God. Judging from Scripture, what is that nature like?

Prayer: That God would make us like Himself, holy as He is holy— Christlike.

Day Two

Today's Verse: "Make a plate of pure gold and engrave on it as on a seal: holy to the Lord." (Exodus 28:36)

Yesterday we talked about the development of the word "holy" after God chose that word to describe Himself. Beyond the initial occurrence in Exodus 3:5 it is used in a variety of ways. Exodus refers to holy convocations, habitations, Sabbaths, a nation, men, places, garments, gifts, crowns, ointment, oil, days, offerings.

Here's the point—things become holy in association with God. Says Dennis Kinlaw:

> Where He is, His presence sanctifies or judges. Without His presence, all is profane. Where His presence is welcomed, His holiness is imparted. Where His presence is rejected, His holiness inexorably brings judgment.[ii]

But note it well—holiness is not simply one among many descriptors of God. It is the fundamental reality of His nature which qualifies all the other attributes.

There is a significant change in how the term "holy" is used from the Old Testament to the New. In the Old, the emphasis is primarily in reference to the holiness of the Almighty. In the New, because the term is now well-established, it speaks of God's will for all believers.

> The God who is holy love has now provided through the atonement of the Holy One, Jesus, and through the sanctifying work of the Spirit, the possibility of likeness unto Him who alone is holy in himself.[iii]

Question: It is possible to claim personal holiness without the actual presence of God. What would holiness without His presence look like?

Prayer: "Where He is, His presence sanctifies." Pray for His unmistakable presence in your life this week, the life of your family, the life of your church.

Day Three

Today's Verse: "Who among the gods is like you, Lord? Who is like you—majestic in holiness, awesome in glory, working wonders?" (Exodus 15:11)

Holiness matters. It is *the* religious term of *all* religious terms or, as scholar J.R. Williams says, it is "the religious term par excellence." Other scholarly perspectives:

- "Holiness is not to be treated as simply another of the attributes of God. If thought of as an attribute, it must be seen as the attribute of attributes, the essence of God's character which determines the nature of His attributes." (Dennis Kinlaw)

- "When the word holy is applied to God, it does not signify one single attribute. ...The word is used as a synonym for his deity." (R.C. Sproul)

- "The word 'holy' is such a fundamental word in religion that 'the Holy One' is accepted as synonymous with God. To say that God is holy is in reality the same as saying that God is God." (Gustaf Aulen)

- "Holiness is not one divine quality among others, even the chiefest, for it expresses what is characteristic of God..." (Edmond Jacob)

- "To be sure He is many things: Justice, Wrath, Love, etc.: but each is always qualified by His holiness, i.e., it is holy justice, holy wrath, or holy love. When Isaiah and John saw their visions of what God was the creatures around the throne were not crying Love, Love, Love: even though love is extremely important..." (Allan Coppedge)

The chief end of man is to "be holy, as He is holy." We are called to reflect God.

Question: Name a dozen or so words that come to your mind when you think of God's awesome holiness.

Prayer: "Lord, you didn't intend for holiness to be just another word. It was special, like you are and you want us to be. Show us how we can be holy, set apart, for You."

Day Four

Today's Verse: "You were washed, you were sanctified, you were justified in the name of the Lord Jesus Christ and by the Spirit of our God." (1 Corinthians 6:9-11)

The day after David Wilkerson of *Teen Challenge* died, author Nancy French wrote quite a remembrance on a blog for the *National Review.* She recalled that the first time she ever attended the church Wilkerson pastored he said,

> "Ladies, when we stand to sing, please don't leave your pocketbooks on the ground. Some thieves are here in the sanctuary, so keep an eye out on your belongings. And for those of you who came here expressly to steal, we welcome you. You came here thinking you'd leave with a few bucks, but you'll leave knowing the life-changing love of God. Stay as long as you'd like."[iv]

What a privileged life in Jesus it would be to attend a church where you knew thieves were ready to do damage, and you welcomed them anyway.

Paul challenges the church at Corinth with these words:

> Do not be deceived: Neither the sexually immoral nor idolaters nor adulterers nor male prostitutes nor homosexual offenders nor thieves nor the greedy nor drunkards nor slanderers nor swindlers will inherit the kingdom of God.

Many of us would give that passage a resounding "Amen!" But Paul goes on in the next sentence to say

> ...that is what some of you were. But you were washed, you were sanctified, you were justified in the name of the Lord Jesus Christ and by the Spirit of our God. (1 Corinthians 6:9-11)

Question: Do you attend a church where adulterers, prostitutes homosexuals, drunkards, slanderers and swindlers are welcome? Why would you want to try to do church without them?

Prayer: "God – may all unholy people feel welcome in our places of worship...so that they might become holy."

Day Five

Today's Verse: "Go into all the world and preach the good news to all creation." (Mark 16:15)

An old seminary friend—Rev. Jorge Acevedo—was speaking at a baccalaureate service I attended. During the sermon he made a very interesting observation: "Jesus' favorite word was 'go.'" I decided to look it up. Try it! You'll find:

> Jesus looked at him and loved him. "One thing you lack," he said. "**Go**, sell everything you have and give to the poor...Then come, follow me." (Mk. 10:21) *A "go" that challenges to radical discipleship.*

> He said to them, "**Go** into all the world and preach the good news to all creation. (Mk. 16:15) *A "go" that is global and encompassing.*

> Therefore **go** and make disciples of all nations, baptizing them in the name of the Father and of the Son and of the Holy Spirit... (Matt. 28:19) *A "go" that is worldwide and disciple-based.*

> Jesus said to him, "Let the dead bury their own dead, but you **go** and proclaim the kingdom of God." (Lk. 9:60) *A "go" that forces the would-be disciple to prioritize. Honor your daddy by not putting him first!*

> **Go!** I am sending you out like lambs among wolves. (Lk. 10:3) *A "go" that is dangerous. And He can be dangerous!*

> The expert in the law replied, "The one who had mercy on him." Jesus told him, "**Go** and do likewise." (Lk. 10:37) *A "go" that calls us to holy response.*

> "Then the owner of the house became angry and ordered his servant, '**Go** out quickly into the streets and alleys of the town and bring in the poor, the crippled, the blind and the lame.' (Lk. 14:21) *A "go" that asks us to invite the 'untouchables' to the party of God.*

> Then he said to him, "Rise and **go**; your faith has made you well." (Luke 17:19) *A "go" that beckons the healed to rise and walk in faith.*

Question: Holiness and "Go" are related. What does the Lord want you to go and do today?

Prayer: Pray to the God on the go that He would make you like Himself—going for the Great Commission and the glory of God.

Day Six

Week One Memory Verse: 1 Peter 1:14-15

Today's Verse: "Who are my mother and my brothers…Whoever does God's will is my brother and sister and mother." (Mark 3:33-34)

There is power in "holy going." I have a friend who, as a senior in high school, got a girl pregnant. She ended up having an abortion. Years later, after a foray in prison (where he found the Lord and was marvelously discipled), he was studying Proverbs and came upon the verse that says "Rescue those being led away to death; hold back those staggering toward slaughter." (24:11)

He felt the Holy Spirit leading him through this verse to the local abortion clinic. He really didn't know what he was doing. He tried to talk to the women but had a relatively fruitless time engaging anybody's attention. He didn't want to be there, but he felt God's nudge nonetheless.

His third week outside the clinic, the lady who ran the place came out and started to give him a piece of her mind. She called him an abortion bomber and otherwise did her best to make him leave the premises. After her tirade, he asked if he could give a little testimony. She listened. He talked about his pregnant girlfriend, of how she visited an abortion clinic without his knowledge, found out the baby was a boy and proceeded to abort him. At the end of the testimony he was in tears and, unlikely as it might seem, so was she.

My friend led her right there, unbelievably, to the Lord. She left the clinic, went on to nursing school and a better future. He obeyed what the Spirit was saying through a passage of Scripture and an abortionist went running into the arms of Jesus.

His story got me to wondering about trying a new Bible study method. Read, and find out based on your responsible observation and interpretation of the Text what fresh thing the Lord is saying and might have you to do…today. Then, go and do it.

Question: From your Scripture reading today, what does the Lord want you to get up and get done?

Prayer: Lord, grant us the courage and wisdom to be holy doers of the Word, and not hearers only.

Day Seven

Week One Memory Verse: 1 Peter 1:14-15

Today's Verse: "After they prayed, the place where they were meeting was shaken. And they were all filled with the Holy Spirit and spoke the word of God boldly. " (Acts 4:31)

More about "going." I once invited a former student to speak in my church. His name was Ghuna, he was from India, and at the end of the service I asked him to help me pray with a visitor. "David (not his real name) here has separated from his wife," I said. "He's moved here to Mississippi and she is in Texas. You want to help us pray?"

At that point, I was no longer needed in the conversation. My friend Ghuna took over. "Where is she?" he asked. "Texas. Texas is a couple states over."

"Yes," said Ghuna, "I know where Texas is. I want to talk to her."

"But you can't, I just told you she is in Texas." Ghuna pointed to David's phone. By this time I was inching away, slightly embarrassed over such brash treatment of a visitor but not quite knowing what to do.

David seemed incredulous, but reluctantly called his wife Debbie (not her real name) and explained that a little Indian man wanted to speak to her. Ghuna took the phone and asked Debbie to tell him the problem with the marriage. All David and I could see was Ghuna thoughtfully nodding and murmuring assents. Ghuna told her good-bye, handed the phone back to David, looked him straight in the eye and said, "It's your fault!"

Before David could protest, Ghuna continued, "I leave on Thursday. I want to meet with you two before then." David raised his eyebrows in disbelief. "She is in Texas." He began his geography lesson once again but Ghuna interrupted. "I know...find a place in Louisiana and we will meet."

Long story short—Ghuna counseled with David and Debbie in a restaurant in Louisiana. Their marriage was reconciled. And that week the student taught the professor about holy leading by the Spirit, holy boldness, and holy confrontation.

Question: How can we know the difference between holy boldness and rudeness?

Prayer: Pray that holiness and "go" will be wed in our lives.

Day Eight

Week Two Memory Verse: Hebrews 12:14 (see p. 62)

Today's Verse: "Again he said, 'What shall we say the kingdom of God is like, or what parable shall we use to describe it?'" (Mark 4:30)

Dr. Allan Coppedge says, "There are many ways to understand the holy God who reveals Himself in Scripture. In His revelation God has chosen to make Himself known in a number of significant roles in order that we might understand the fullness of His being and character."

So, Coppedge has identified eight major word pictures that God has used to show Himself to us. "The fact that God chose a number of major portraits in order to make Himself known is important. It means that while He is like all these, He is not to be perfectly identified with any single one of them. Each role is valuable, but has limits, and no one of them can be made to stand alone or pressed too far without distorting the picture of what God is really like."

For each portrait there is a way of understanding many aspects of our relationship to God, not the least various ways of looking at sin, salvation and entire sanctification. So, depending on your theological background and your experiences there might be one or just a few of these that resonate with how you have perceived God in the past and in the present. Our growth in the Christian faith demands, however, that we not only acknowledge the portrait with which we are most comfortable with but also strengthen our understanding by examining other portraits.

The Portraits of our Holy God

Stage	Good Shepherd	Sovereign King	Loving Father	Transcendent Creator
Sin	Wandering	Rebellion	Self-love / Disobedience	Marred image / idolatry
Salvation	Found	Forgiveness	New birth / Life	Regeneration/ Life
Entire sanctification	Total following / rest of faith	Full submission / Lordship	Perfect love	Full remake of image

Stage	Personal Revealer	Righteous Judge	Powerful Redeemer	Pure Priest
Sin	Rejection of truth	Lawless / transgression	Bondage / imprisonment	Defilement / Unclean
Salvation	Reception of Christ and teachings	Justification	Redemption / ransom / deliverance	Forgiveness / cleansing
Entire sanctification	Walking fully in truth	Full obedience / blamelessness	Full redemption	Full cleansing / purification

I see my own testimony in terms of the "Good Shepherd" category. I was wandering, He found me and now I am, by His grace, resting in Him and by His grace following fully. Conversely, I respond to the "Righteous Judge" and "Pure Priest" categories least, for various reasons. I need extra exposure to them.

How about you? What is the portrait that best describes your faith journey? Which pictures of God need strengthening in your understanding?

I have found these portraits of great use in my prayer life. I will take one of these per day and meditate on it at my devotional hour and through the day. If I were thinking in terms of "Sovereign King" I would *praise* the King, *confess* to Him my rebellion (in the past and, ongoing, if that be the case), *thank* Him for forgiveness, *meditate* on what full submission and Lordship might mean in my life's situations and *ask* that my family and my church would be active for His Kingdom.

The title of Coppedge's book is *Portraits of God: A Biblical Theology of Holiness.*[v] And, as he would attest, it is a theology of holiness that ought to lead us deeper in God by not only its portraits but also the implications of those eight roles of God in and through our lives.

Questions: At the time of your conversion, which portrait best described your understanding of the faith?

Prayer: Ask that God would paint these portraits across your soul.

Day Nine

Today's Verse: "Worship the Lord in the splendor of his holiness; tremble before him, all the earth." (Psalm 96:9)

God appears harsh, sometimes. The first chapter of Romans is one of those places. God hands people over...just gives them up!

> [24] Therefore God *gave them over* in the sinful desires of their hearts to sexual impurity...

> [26] ...God *gave them over* to shameful lusts.

> [28] ... God...*gave them over* to a depraved mind, to do what ought not to be done.

The word for "gave them over" in the Greek is *paradidomai* (pare–uh–DID–oh–my) and it is variously translated..."gave them up" (KJV), "abandoned them" (NLT), "delivered them over" (HCSB).

Dr. Carl Henry, one of the preeminent theologians of the 20th century, suggested that *paradidomai* was one of the most thunderous words of the New Testament. He then made a startling observation: he wondered whether or not God had already done this very thing to America.

> I think we are now living in the very decade when God may thunder his awesome *paradidomai* (I abandon, or I give [them] up) (Rom. 1:24 ff.) over America's professed greatness. Our massacre of a million fetuses a year; our deliberate flight from the monogamous family; our normalizing, of fornication and of homosexuality and other sexual perversion; our programming of self-indulgence above social and familial concerns—all represent a quantum leap in moral deterioration, a leap more awesome than even the supposed qualitative gulf between conventional weapons and nuclear missiles. Our nation has all but tripped the worst ratings on God's Richter scale of fully deserved moral judgment.[vi]

I am reminded of Anne Graham Lotz' comments once on "The Early Show." Jane Clayson asked her (regarding Hurricane Katrina), "How could God let something like this happen?"

> She said: "I believe God is deeply saddened by this, just as we are, but for years we've been telling God to get out of our schools, to get out of our government and to get out of our lives. And being the gentleman He is, I believe He has calmly backed out. How can we expect God to give us His blessing and His protection if we demand He leave us alone?"

God is the quintessential Holy Gentleman. If we continually tell Him to leave us alone, should we be surprised that this is what He will do?

Questions: God is holy which means, among many other things, He is capable of harsh responses. What has humankind ever done to deserve His harsh response? What you have *you* ever done to deserve Him *giving you up*?

Prayer Request: "Holy Father, you can hand us over and give us up. Forgive us, and give us grace to repent so such a thing is never done to us, our families or our nation."

Day Ten

Week Two Memory Verse: Hebrews 12:14

Today's Verse: "Speak to the entire assembly of Israel and say to them: 'Be holy because I, the LORD your God, am holy.'" (Leviticus 19:2)

How do the Old and New testaments fit together?   Dr. John Oswalt said once that "The New Testament answers the question the Old Testament asks."

Now, some have thought that the big-ticket question of the Bible was "How can we make it into heaven?" But if Oswalt is right, the question of the Old Testament cannot be how to get into heaven because the Old Testament has no concept of heaven. It just isn't there.   Since we got the question wrong, we answer poorly. Unfortunately, we have devised a contemporary evangelicalism on the foundation of an inaccurate question.

So—what is the query of the Old Testament?

"How can we be holy, as He is holy?"

Stated another way: "How can we live a life reflective of the goodness and awesomeness and lovingkindness and righteousness of our God?"

The New Testament has the answer, and the Testaments read together start resonating as a coherent whole. How can we be holy? Well, God has to take action, for we cannot make ourselves holy. So—God takes a personal course of action.

We become holy as God 1) comes, 2) teaches, 3) dies, 4) is resurrected and then 5) sends the Spirit to live in and through us. The right question explains the mission of God in the New Testament and begins to shift our thinking from "How can I get to heaven?" to "How can I get heaven/holiness into me, and others, that we might reflect Him?"

Questions: How is "How can I get to heaven" an inadequate question? What could be distorted if this becomes our main concern?

Prayer Request: "'Heaven into us'—this is what we want, dear Lord. Help us to never accept anything less."

Day Eleven

Today's Verse: "Therefore, prepare your minds for action; be self-controlled; set your hope fully on the grace to be given you when Jesus Christ is revealed. As obedient children, do not conform to the evil desires you had when you lived in ignorance. But just as he who called you is holy, so be holy in all you do; For it is written, 'Be holy, because I am holy.'" (1 Peter 1:13-16)

"The fate of the Christian Church in America and around the world depends upon what the Church does with the biblical doctrine of holiness," says John Oswalt.[vii] Peter, under the direction of the Holy Spirit, gives us the passage quoted above in "today's verse" to remind us that God's grace is most certainly linked to a radically transformed life. To claim to have received God's gift of salvation while continuing to live a life obviously dominated by the temptations of the world is a contradiction in terms.

So...what is the holiness of which we speak? What is Peter talking about?

> 1) Holiness first of all defines a way of behaving; 2) It is a way of behaving which is determined by the character of God; 3) It is a way of behaving which all Christians are expected to manifest; and 4) It is a way of behaving which is markedly different from that of unbelievers.[viii]

Holy living is the outcome in our lives of the Holy Bible, the Holy One of Israel, the Holy Spirit and the holy, holy, holy vision of heaven pronounced in the accounts of Isaiah and John's revelation.

But Oswalt is right; holiness impacts what a person does and doesn't do. The work in the heart has its fruit in one's behavior.

Questions: Why do people want the promise of heaven from our Holy God without the promise of a totally transformed life from that same God?

Prayer Request: Pray for a transformed life, family, church that we might be holy as He is holy.

Day Twelve

Today's Verse: "For he chose us in him before the creation of the world to be holy and blameless in his sight. In love he predestined us for adoption to sonship through Jesus Christ, in accordance with his pleasure and will—" (Ephesians 1:4-5)

"How little people know who think that holiness is dull," wrote C.S. Lewis to a friend in America. "When one meets the real thing...it is irresistible. If even 10 percent of the world's population had it, would not the whole world be converted and happy before the year's end?"

It is probably fair to say that when most people think of the word "holiness," the term "exciting" rarely comes to mind. Samuel Miller's words might explain our dilemma:

> He was careless about himself, we are careful. He was courageous, we are cautious. He trusted the untrustworthy, we trust those who have good collateral. He forgave the unforgiveable, we forgive those who do not really hurt us. He was righteous and laughed at respectability, we are respectable and smile at righteousness. He was meek, we are ambitious. He saved others, we save ourselves as much as we can. He had no place to lay his head, and did not worry about it, while we fret because we do not have the last convenience manufactured by clever science. He did what he believed to be right regardless of consequences, while we determine what is right by how it will affect us. He feared God, but not the world. We fear public opinion more than we fear the judgment of God. He risked everything for God, we make religion a refuge from every risk. He took up the cross, we neither take it up nor lay it down, but merely let it stand.[ix]

A life lived for Jesus can be exceedingly dangerous. But dangerous or not, none should call it anything less than exciting. What we dare not end up being is boring, dry, predictable, stale—for whatever holiness is, it is not that.

Question: How are we capable of making holiness dull?

Prayer Request: "Jesus, make us as exciting as you."

Day Thirteen

Week Two Memory Verse: Hebrews 12:14

Today's Verse: "Who among the gods is like you, Lord? Who is like you—majestic in holiness, awesome in glory, working wonders? " (Exodus 15:11)

The Rev. David W. Preus, bishop emeritus of the former American Lutheran Church, stood before a group of graduate students at Luther Northwestern Theological Seminary in St. Paul, Minnesota. He had some disturbing news to report:

> After 39 years of being a pastor, I have to say that our greatest public sin is that we are boring. Our sermons are not so heretical as they are uninteresting. We distrust excitement, and we are not even sure about enthusiasm….A visitor at our worship services is likely to figure that the most exciting part is trying to figure out where you are between bulletin and hymnal, standing and sitting, and passing the collection plate.[x]

Compare that to a recent church service I attended at a church in what some would refer to as a "holiness" denomination. There was upbeat music pointing the congregation to the face of their Savior. A time of greeting while the mixed race crowd warmly welcomed each other, followed by a congregational recitation of their mission statement to be transformed by Jesus and released to fulfill God's mission in their community and around the world. Then, after affirming their corporate commitment to daily prayer and study, service inside the church and out, giving sacrificially and missions, the crowd was invited to the altar for prayer and healing. There was a message of transformational challenge from Scripture. Then the service ended with the baptism of four prisoners.

Boring? No. Missional, exciting and enthusiastic? Yes. We should be reminded that the early Methodists with their penchant for holiness were derisively chalked up as *enthusiasts*. It was because growth, holiness and vibrancy tended to reflect their life together.

Questions: What could be a definition of the phrase, "holy excitement?" How do you think Jesus would describe it?

Prayer Request: "Holy Spirit, make us exciting, enthusiastic and upbeat as you work in, and through, us."

Day Fourteen

Week Two Memory Verse: Hebrews 12:14

Today's Verse: "My heart says of you, 'Seek his face!' Your face, Lord, I will seek. " (Psalm 27:8)

Nathaniel Hawthorne's short story "The Great Stone Face" centers around a man named Ernest who grew up in a village renowned for a natural wonder that rested just outside its boundaries. Nature had majestically carved in the side of a mountain the features of a human visage so realistic that from a distance the Great Stone Face appeared to be alive.

Ernest was told of an ancient prophecy that at some future day a child would be born in the vicinity who would himself grow up to resemble the Stone Face. Ernest, fascinated, mediated upon the countenance, looked to it for solace, read stories about it and became the village expert on this natural wonder.

Years passed. Imposters periodically appeared, proclaiming themselves to be the Face. Each time Ernest would look and each time walk away crestfallen. "Fear not," the rock seemed to say, "the man will come."

One day, late in his life, Ernest was giving an eloquent oration upon the Great Stone Face. A poet in the crowd grew teary-eyed, for he felt in the moment that Ernest's words were nobler by far than any poetry he had ever written. Suddenly, with the Stone Face looming in the background, the poet was moved by an irresistible impulse to throw his arms aloft and shout to all who would hear—"Behold, behold! Ernest is himself the likeness of the Great Stone Face!"

Ernest had become like his ideal.

Holiness starts here: what gets our attention gets us. We grow to resemble that which captures our hearts and minds.

Questions: What is your ideal? How are you becoming like that ideal?

Prayer: "Help us, O Lord, to seek Your face. Teach us what it means to be consumed with a desire to know and love You more."

Day Fifteen

Week Three Memory Verse: Matthew 22:37 (see p. 62)

Today's Verse: "Be holy, because I am holy." (I Peter 1:16)

Peter wrote to the fellow Christians of his day these rather prominent Old Testament thoughts.

"Be holy as I am holy" is quite a challenge from God! For the serious inquirer, it begs the question—What is God like?

E. Stanley Jones, great Methodist missionary, said, "The greatest thing that can be said of God or man is that that being is Christlike." Jesus is one of the Persons of what orthodox Christianity claims is the three-person God, but He is obviously the clearest picture of what a Holy One looks like in the flesh.

That is not all that can or will be articulated on the subject, but it is the best, clearest and highest thing that can be said.

The Old Testament concept of holy comes from the Hebrew word *qadosh*. This term and related words appear over 600 times in the Old Testament, and an entire book (Leviticus) is committed the early treatment of this subject. Indeed, Leviticus was so significant to the Jewish people that children were taught to read from that book. It was important for them to know from the get-go what it meant to approach a Holy God.

In an incomplete nutshell, here it is: A Holy God is

- love, *(Dt. 7:7-9)*,
- different *(Lev. 11:44-45)*,
- awesome *(Gen. 28:17)*,
- sacred *(Ex. 3:5)*,
- majestic *(Ex. 15:11)*,
- separate *(Hos. 11:9)*,
- pure *(Ps. 24:3-4)*,
- unique and incomparable *(I Sam. 2:2; 6:20; Isa. 40:18-26; Hab. 3:3)*
- just *(Ps. 99:3-5)*,
- hater of sin *(Dt. 7:10)* and
- lover of cleanliness *(Ez. 36:23-35)*.

Other terms and scriptures could obviously be added; this is, after all, a big subject. For instance, E. Stanley Jones describes the Sermon on the Mount as the self-portrait of Jesus. The beatitudes kick off that sermon.

> Poor in spirit
> Mournful
> Meek
> Hungering and thirsting for righteousness
> Merciful
> Pure in heart
> Peacemaker
> Persecuted for the sake of righteousness

Jesus was saying, "This is what I am like; follow my example."

Paul seemed to be describing holiness when he offered the fruit of the Spirit:

> Love
> Joy
> Peace
> Patience
> Kindness
> Goodness
> Faithfulness
> Gentleness
> Self-control

None of these lists is exhaustive, of course, but a brief rendition of what holiness should be for the believer. But here's an insight not to miss: In the Hebrew language, the opposite of holy is "common," which is the same word for "profane." *Common* equals *profane* in God's ancient language of choice.

Lord, make us different.

Question: What, do you suppose, was so wrong in the Lord's eyes with being "common"?

Prayer: "Holy Spirit, make us different. Not just any kind of different, but *holy* different."

Day Sixteen

Today's Verse: "And they were calling to one another: 'Holy, holy, holy is the LORD Almighty; the whole earth is full of his glory.'" (Exodus 15:11)

In the Old Testament once God starts to communicate His nature to Moses and to the redeemed nation the usage of the terms related to holiness explodes. There are over 830 instances of this term in all its forms in the Old Testament. The study of holiness, then, can get a bit lengthy and complicated.

Some years ago we were putting together a children's catechism. One of the statements to be memorized defined a commandment as "a law of God." Simple enough. We submitted this question and answer to a friend, Dr. Bill Ury, for critique. His edit? He scribbled out our answer and gave this one:

> "A commandment is a picture of who God is
> and a promise of what we can become!"

I've never looked at a biblical directive in the same way since.

One day, Jesus is asked by an expert in the law "Which is the greatest commandment in the Law?" Jesus replied: "Love the Lord your God with all your heart and with all your soul and with all your mind'....the second is like it: 'Love your neighbor as yourself.' All the Law and the Prophets hang on these two commandments."

John Wesley would come along some seventeen centuries later and say that those two commandments highlighted by Jesus were the gist of what holiness is all about. A picture of who God was in the flesh, and a promise of what we could become. Love, personified.

Questions: Which is harder—loving God or loving neighbor? Why?

Prayer: Pray that God would help you live today into this great definition of holiness to—love God and love neighbor.

Day Seventeen

Today's Verse: "But the Advocate, the Holy Spirit, whom the Father will send in my name, will teach you all things and will remind you of everything I have said to you." (John 14:26)

The Holy Spirit makes people holy! The Spirit teaches, guides, empowers, convicts of sin, fills, etc. But all for the purpose of *making us holy*. The Holy Spirit recreates people to be like God in His moral character.

My wife and I once held a Quaker "quiet meeting" in our home. To prepare for this service from another tradition, we sent out invitations containing three rules: 1) Don't come planning to say anything, 2) Don't come planning to say nothing and 3) Do nothing to draw attention to yourself. I explained to the assembled that once the meeting began we would all enter into a time of silence. Then, as the Spirit moved, someone might sing, or recite poetry, or preach; or perhaps we might spend the whole hour and a half in silence. God can choose to speak through that means, too. We just needed to quiet ourselves, listen and respond.

After I prayed, we all entered into a time of what seemed to be interminable silence. About fifteen minutes in—an eternity it seemed! —my buddy Ellis began to sing quietly:

> He is here, He is here, and He's moving among us.
> He is here, He is here as we gather in His name.
> He is here, He is here, and He wants to work a wonder
> He is here as we gather in His name.

The Spirit *was* there! And He has reminded me ever since that where His "wonder" is, holiness abides. Sometimes He works quietly; sometimes He bursts upon the scene. Sometimes He heals, sometimes He blesses us in persecution. But always, always, the Holy One makes holy.

Question: What is the typical response when someone asks, "What does the Holy Spirit do for us?"

Prayer: "Spirit, whatever you do, make me holy. Then work through me that others might have the same experience."

Day Eighteen

Today's Verse: "You were taught, with regard to your former way of life, to put off your old self, which is being corrupted by its deceitful desires; to be made new in the attitude of your minds; and to put on the new self, created to be like God in true righteousness and holiness." (Ephesians 4:22-23)

Historically, few people have been more interested in the topic of holiness and its impact on the believer than was John Wesley. He wanted the early Methodists to know that holiness had very practical, very real, and very challenging ramifications. In his volume *A Plain Account of Christian Perfection* he defined the "Character of a Methodist."

> Loves God with all his heart, soul, mind and strength.
> In everything gives thanks
> Heart lifted to God at all times
> Loves every man as his own soul
> Pure in heart
> God reigns alone in his life
> Keeps all the commandments
> Does all to the glory of God
> Adorns the doctrine of God in all things

This is a pretty good checklist for anyone wanting to talk in terms of specific characteristics or shortcomings in their own life. And Wesley was serious about such matters. While love was the attribute most evidently taught in early Methodism, accountability was also a watchword. Wesley developed "bands"—small groups where participants asked tough and incisive questions of each other in order to promote holy living. Some resisted then; some will resist that kind of intense interrogation now.

But holiness is a high calling. Do we love the holiness of God enough, and desire it earnestly enough for our own lives, to seek the face of a Holy God and practice holy means and measures?

Question: Look through Wesley's list. Which is the strongest/weakest in your life?

Prayer: "Examine me, Lord, through the use of good questions applied to my soul."

Day Nineteen

Week Three Memory Verse: Matthew 22:37

Today's Verse: "But we ought always to thank God for you, brothers and sisters loved by the Lord, because God chose you as firstfruits to be saved through the sanctifying work of the Spirit and through belief in the truth." (2 Thessalonians 2:13)

Read Ephesians and guess what Paul's "trigger word/concept/topic is.

> For this reason I, Paul, the prisoner of Christ Jesus for the sake of you *Gentiles*—

That hyphen, and the subsequent explanation, lasts for a chapter. Paul picks up where he left off at the top of chapter four. But "Gentiles" is what really revs Paul's motor. Before that fourth chapter he talks about the mystery given to him—the *Gentiles* are heirs together with Israel. And Paul aims to let them know that no matter how much trouble, turmoil, beatings, heartache and assorted other suffering it costs him to let them and his fellow Jews know grace, his life will be thus poured out.

I tell my students at the seminary that while they are studying Bible and theology, ancient languages and sacraments, history and philosophy—remember to ask God to grant them a "holy trigger." In other words, let God put on their heart some people or area of the world where they see a desperate need and thus want to pour their lives out that the Gospel might impact the heart-wrenching misery found there.

If we don't have this, we run the risk of our hearts curving in on themselves, concerned for OUR salvation and OUR needs and OUR agendas and OUR hopes and OUR pilgrimage to heaven.

Question: What is your "trigger word?" To whom is your heart curved outward?

Prayer: "Jesus, reveal Yourself and the people/place you specifically want on my heart. Then give me the fortitude to wholeheartedly move toward this calling. Amen."

Day Twenty

Today's Verse: "And in fact, you do love all the brothers throughout Macedonia. Yet we urge you, brothers, to do so more and more." (1 Thess. 4:10)

Paul liked certain phrases. "More and more" was one of them. For instance:

> All this is for your benefit, so that the grace that is reaching **more and more** people may cause thanksgiving to overflow to the glory of God. (2 Cor. 4:15)

> And this is my prayer: that your love may abound **more and more** in knowledge and depth of insight... (Philippians 1:9)

In his letters to the Thessalonians he warmed up even more to the words:

> Finally, brothers, we instructed you how to live in order to please God, as in fact you are living. Now we ask you and urge you in the Lord Jesus to do this **more and more**. (1 Thess. 4:1)

> And in fact, you do love all the brothers throughout Macedonia. Yet we urge you, brothers, to do so **more and more**. (1 Thess. 4:10)

> We ought always to thank God for you, brothers, and rightly so, because your faith is growing **more and more**, and the love every one of you has for each other is increasing. (2 Thess. 1:3)

The Greek term for "more and more" was one word, two syllables—*mallon* (MAH-lon)— which meant "to a greater quantity, larger measure, higher degree and sooner rather than later." In brief, in "living to please God" and in "love" and in "growing faith" Paul wanted the house church in Thessalonica to step on the proverbial accelerator. Keep it up! Keep going! Greater! Larger! Higher! Because where does all this finally lead, this more-and-more-ness?

To through-and-throughness! The apostle wraps up the first epistle to these dear saints with these words:

> May God himself, the God of peace, sanctify you **through and through**. May your whole spirit, soul and body be kept blameless at

the coming of our Lord Jesus Christ. The one who calls you is faithful and he will do it. (1 Thess. 5:23-24)

Before Paul signs off in his first Epistle to the saints in Thessalonica he wants them to know where "more" leads. It eventually encompasses all of who we are. God changes the "more," by His grace, into a total invasion.

There is, of course, a more-and-moreness that does quite the opposite, and Paul warns his young disciple Timothy about it.

Avoid godless chatter, because those who indulge in it will become **more and more** ungodly. (2 Tim. 2:16)

One can imagine, then, where more and more ungodliness leads...to through and through wickedness.

Question: Anything in your Christian life you would like to have more of?

Prayer: "Lord, each day we choose what kind of 'more' we want. Keep us sober in our choices, knowing where the 'more' leads. Amen."

Day Twenty-One

Week Three Memory Verse: Matthew 22:37

Today's Verse: "He must manage his own family well and see that his children obey him, and he must do so in a manner worthy of full respect. " (1 Timothy 3:4)

When your church seeks a pastor or leader, what is the number one criterion you look for? Good preacher? Good interpersonal skills? Good lookin'?

It probably won't surprise you to know that the Apostle Paul had an opinion on this one. He wrote to Timothy and to Titus about such things. And He had a nice-sized list he wanted these protégés and their churches to consider:

▪ Able to teach	▪ Not a lover of money
▪ Above reproach—blameless	▪ Not a recent convert
▪ Temperate	▪ Good reputation with
▪ Self-controlled	outsiders
▪ Hospitable	▪ Not overbearing
▪ Not violent but gentle	▪ Not quick-tempered
▪ Respectable	▪ Loves what is good
▪ Does not pursue dishonest	▪ Upright, holy
gain	▪ Disciplined
▪ Holds to the truth	▪ Sincere
▪ Not quarrelsome	▪ Tested

The list is a good spiritual check for just about anybody (not just potential leadership!). But the list is not quite complete. Because omitted from the above list are these items:

- Husband of one wife
  (Elder: 1 Ti. 3:2; Tit. 1:6)
  (Deacon: 1 Ti. 3:12)

- Obedient children
  (Elder: 1 Ti. 3:4-5; Tit. 1:6)
  (Deacon: 1 Ti. 3:12)

- Manages own family well
  (1 Ti. 3:4, 3:12)

What got the most attention in the early church (both in number of times mentioned and number of words devoted to the characteristics) was the leader's family.

Should we be surprised at such concern over one of the most fundamental relationships in life?

Remember that before the world began, the Bible teaches there was Father and Son—a family.

Could it be that the well-ordered family is God's divine teaching tool to show onlookers what He is like? To the church at Ephesus and Colossae Paul would write more about this family unit...things like "Husbands, love" and "Wives, submit" and "Children, obey." When such attitudes are expressed based on the example and teaching of the Father and Son, then there is holy witness. And where there is holy witness, there is increased chance that "God's will be done on earth as it is in heaven."

Question: What does the Lord need to do to further sanctify (make holy) your family?

Prayer: "Lord, order our families according to your will and character which, of course, is holy."

Day Twenty-Two

Week Four Memory Verse: John 8:34-36 (see p. 62)

Today's Verse: "My eyes will be on the faithful in the land, that they may dwell with me; the one whose walk is blameless will minister to me." (Psalm 101:6)

My two youngest sons were reflecting at the family dinner table over the Mary and Martha narrative. Martha is hustling around trying to get the house in order for Jesus. Mary is actually sitting at His feet and listening to Him. So, I queried the boys—what is the moral of this story?

My boys went a little deeper than the typical analysis when they concluded: "She focused on Jesus 'in the moment.'" (Luke 10:42)

For all those who insist that this narrative means we should slow down, chill out and sit at Jesus' feet—well, did you ever notice the story that precedes the Martha and Mary narrative? It is the story of the Good Samaritan, where one guy sees another guy in dire straits and makes a heroic physical effort (not to mention expensive!) to deal with the situation. Jesus concludes at the end of that story that His challenger should "go and do likewise."

What was the Good Samaritan doing? Focusing on Jesus in the moment. Christ taught that there would be blessing for those who were experientially and very practically busy with people in their moments of crisis: "I was hungry…I was thirsty…I was a stranger…needing clothes…I was in prison…and you came to Me—whatever you did for one of the least of these brothers of mine, you did for Me." (Mt. 25:31-46)

The two stand-outs in these stories were those focusing on Jesus in the moment, and apparently three who weren't. Sometimes that focus will include an extraordinary amount of work; at other times it will mean relaxing and opening wide our hearts.

Most of all, it means being with Jesus. Really, really, being with Him. In the moment. Holiness requires it.

Question: What does it mean for you today to focus on Jesus "in the moment"?

Prayer: "Lord, let me see You, really see You, where You are in my day."

Day Twenty-Three

Week Four Memory Verse: John 8:34-36

Today's Verse: "Look to the Lord and His strength; seek His face always."
(Psalm 105:4)

Some years ago, a prominent pastor was asked in a television interview about America and revival. He noted that there was no revival in the American bicentennial year of 1976 or any subsequent years because, frankly, we were too busy seeking God's hand, not His face. Apparently there's a difference.

Most prayer meetings I have attended seek God's hand in their personal and collective lives. Nothing wrong with this, of course, unless we neglect other dynamics of the life of prayer so prominent in Scripture. Seeking His face in praise and adoration certainly seems to be an essential center for our communication with God. If we "major" in praise and adoration it is only natural to go to God with the rest—confession, thanksgiving and supplication.

People who accentuate praise and adoration of that "Face" on a daily and on-going basis have a "glow" about them. They radiate holiness!

Screwtape, the devil, in C.S. Lewis's *The Screwtape Letters* tutors his nephew Wormwood in all things evil. At one point he tells his protégé: "Our cause is never more in danger than when a human, no longer desiring, but still intending, to do our Enemy's will, looks round upon a universe from which every trace of Him seems to have vanished, and asks why he has been forsaken, and still obeys."[xi]

Substitute "obeys" with "seeks His face" and you get the gist of holiness.

Question: How should we seek His face today—what would that mean for us?

Prayer: "Lord, I have prayed for many things. Let me now concentrate, most of all, on You."

Day Twenty-Four

Week Four Memory Verse: John 8:34-36

Today's Verse: "I want to know Christ—yes, to know the power of his resurrection and participation in his sufferings, becoming like him in his death..." (Philippians 3:10)

In the last several years, many in evangelicalism have decided that a Christian worldview is what we really need; without it, we are lost. One can understand the concern.

The celebrated researcher George Barna produced a bevy of disheartening statistics showing evangelicals' lack of belief in simple biblical orthodoxy (correct doctrine). For instance, in recent studies...

- Nearly half of self-described born again Christians (47%) agree that Satan is "not a living being but is a symbol of evil."

- A majority of all born again Christians reject the existence of the Holy Spirit (55%).

- 4% of Christians and 3% of non-Christians said they had consulted a medium or spiritual advisor, other than a minister, within the past month.

- 31% of "born-agains" also believe that if a person is good enough they can earn a place in Heaven.

- 24% of "born-agains" agree that "while he lived on earth, Jesus committed sins, like other people," compared to half (49%) of non-Christians.

- About one out of four (26%) "born-again" Christians believe that it doesn't matter what faith you follow because they all teach the same lessons; a belief held by 56% of non-Christians.

So...let's get our orthodoxy straight. That will make us all good Christians, right?

John Wesley didn't think so.

> ...neither does religion consist in Orthodoxy, or right opinions; which, although they are not properly outward things, are not in the heart, but the understanding.
>
> A man may be orthodox in every point; he may not only espouse right opinions, but zealously defend them against all opposers; he may think justly concerning the incarnation of our Lord, concerning the ever-blessed Trinity, and every other doctrine contained in the oracles of God; he may assent to all the three creeds, —that called the Apostles', the Nicene, and the Athanasian; and yet it is possible he may have no religion at all, no more than a Jew, Turk, or pagan.
>
> He may be almost as orthodox—as the devil, (though, indeed, not altogether; for every man errs in something; whereas we can't well conceive him to hold any erroneous opinion,) and may, all the while be as great a stranger as he to the religion of the heart.
>
> This alone is religion, truly so called: This alone is in the sight of God of great price. The Apostle sums it all up in three particulars, "righteousness, and peace, and joy in the Holy Ghost." (Romans 14:7) (Sermon 7—"The Way to the Kingdom")

The position here is clear—we can be "orthodox" to the hilt and yet be lost as lost can be.

The "heart" is key to right standing with God. Jesus looks at our heart, not primarily our worldview. This is not to say, of course, that "worldview" or "orthodoxy" are not incredibly important. But we can "know" right things and still not be "saved by grace through faith in Christ Jesus."

"Heart" includes the "seat of the mind, of the emotions and of the will." It is a full-orbed term. But Wesley also knew this—faith is more than just being intellectually convinced of biblical tenets. Our whole lives must be His.

Question: Is there anything we are "intellectually" convinced of that we don't live out in our day-to-day living?

Prayer: "Lord, make my beliefs more than intellectual...may my beliefs be as the Kingdom—'righteousness, peace and joy in the Holy Spirit' —and may they impact my mind, my feelings, my will. And let me truly live accordingly."

Day Twenty-Five

Today's Verse: "...showing all good faith so that they will adorn the doctrine of God our Savior in every respect." (Titus 2:10/NASB)

Paul writes to Titus on the island of Crete and instructs his protégé to "straighten out what was left unfinished..." One of the things the apostle tells Titus is to "Teach slaves to be subject to their masters in everything, to try to please them, not to talk back to them, and not to steal from them, but to show that they can be fully trusted, so that in every way they will make the teaching about God our Savior attractive." (Titus 2:9-10)

A strange turn of a phrase—"make the teaching about God...attractive." In the slave's case, the road to attractiveness would be paved by

- submission,
- doing good work,
- being willing to be quiet when transgressed against,
- honesty and
- trustworthiness.

For those of us in other settings, how might that list be further expanded? A small start...

- Love (a commitment to be God's conduit of kindness)
- Compassion (reaching out to those around us with holy empathy)
- Joy (take life's toughest licks with pluck and buoyancy)
- Perseverance ("hang in there" with tough people and situations)

Keith Miller once wrote a book called *The Scent of Love*. Its thesis was this: if the Body of Christ would act like Christ, what a beautiful scent would enter the cultural atmosphere. An appealing verbal presentation of Christ is important. More important still are attractive character and community. And the word for that kind of beauty is...holiness.

Question: How have you found non-Christians are attracted to Christ through our lives?

Prayer: "Give me that grace that makes difficult things attractive, O God, that I might present your gospel with every word I utter and every decision I make and every act I perform and every gift I give. "

Day Twenty-Six

Today's Verse: "Repent at my rebuke! Then I will pour out my thoughts to you, I will make known to you my teachings." (Proverbs 1:23)

I was out at the detention center tonight, where I preach most Monday evenings. A guy walked up to me and immediately looked familiar. He said he was a *DaySpringer,* an attender of our church (*DaySpring* Community Church).

Interesting circumstance, as the reader might imagine. You love being the pastor of a guy who is down on his luck and battling the tough things in life. Ex-prisoners and others similarly struggling are exactly the kind of guy any evangelistic preacher would want in his church.

It is the kind of "clientele" we live for, or ought to.

I was thrilled to see him. A glad reunion. Glad, that is, until it dawned on me that he was, of course, a prisoner again. If I weren't so slow I would have understood that immediately upon seeing him. In other words, his being a fan and attender of my church meant, alas, that something had gone wrong with the discipleship program of which he was supposedly a part.

What happened?

He showed me his huge scar, the result of heart by-pass surgery. After the surgery, they had given him a pill to assuage the pain. Not good, for a drug addict. That dose led him down a path that landed him right back where I had met him the first time before he came to my church, got sick, took a pill, and ended up where he never wanted to find himself again.

No excuses, of course, and he knew it. He wasn't trying to make one. But he was telling me his story, and there it was.

I reflected on our conversation as I drove home from that facility. How many times do we take a proverbial "pill" and, thinking we will be helped by it, instead find ourselves facedown against the hard surface of life's gravel road? It might have been an actual pill, or something we did for fun, or comfort, or to allay a hunger. It was meant to help, or soothe, or promote, or heal...but it ended up disastrously because we didn't understand or care to consider our personal weakness or addictive tendency.

I have known a few friends who, cognizant of their addiction, said "no" to pain medication before or after a surgery because they understood the potential for harm. They knew that while it would be rough to get through post-surgical discomfort without the conventional treatment prescribed by the experts, spiraling into addiction would be rougher still. It was a risk they chose not to take.

When I was in high school, my dad found out I had been betting on some football games. He sat me down for a man-to-man talk and told me not to gamble. In the course of that conversation, he warned that one of our patriarchs had nearly gambled his life away. The intimation was that something built into our DNA didn't handle well the urge to lay down more money than we should for something not really worth having.

If we did, we might find ourselves in a bad place in life. I have never laid down so much as a nickel for any kind of "gaming" since.

Dad was saying, in essence, that I should "deny myself, take up my cross and follow" Jesus. Not usually fun, this life of denial and cross-bearing. But knowing the alternatives, the call to sacrificial responsibility and holy living is one well worth answering.

Question: What are the hardest things to say "No" to in our lives?

Prayer: "Lord, you are our divine Yes. Help us to also know divine no's."

Day Twenty-Seven

Week Four Memory Verse: John 8:34-36

Today's Verse: "Our Father in heaven, hallowed be Your name." (Matthew 6:9)

The Lord's Prayer contains several powerful lines, and none more potent than this one:

> Thy kingdom come, Thy will be done
> On earth as it is in heaven.

This passage potentially evokes several responses. Two basic ones would be:

1. Quaint, but impossible.
2. Jesus meant what He said.

This text was one of thirty which John Wesley used to teach on the entire sanctification of believers. But does it mean His will be done on earth as it is in heaven concerning *my* heart? Or in this or that situation that I face in my life today?

This phrase alone should be readily on our lips throughout the day—*Thy Kingdom come, Thy will be done* right here, right now, in this God-given predicament or situation.

Imagine the possibilities not only for personal requests but societal ones: His kingdom come, His will be done for our prison system, the sex-trafficking in our city, the abortion clinics, the strip clubs, the unchurched of this apartment complex, or the unevangelized in that school system.

These ought to be, as they were for Wesley, prayers that move us to trust, and action. A prayer like Jesus' ought to be applied to our personal lives first, but it certainly shouldn't end there.

Question: What is one thing Jesus wants accomplished today that I can (and will) do by His grace?

Prayer: Pray for divine energy to surge through you to get up and do what He wants you to do.

Day Twenty-Eight

Week Four Memory Verse: John 8:34-36

Today's Verse: "Be perfect, therefore, as your heavenly Father is perfect." (Matthew 5:48)

As noted before John Wesley repeatedly based his doctrine of entire sanctification on thirty seminal texts. Five of them came from the relatively tiny letter of the apostle John to Christians in Asia Minor who were undoubtedly being challenged and troubled by false teachers.

> 1 John 1:5, 7: This is the message we have heard from him and declare to you: God is light; in him there is *no darkness at all*. 7 But if we walk in the light, as he is in the light, we have fellowship with one another, and the blood of Jesus, his Son, *purifies us from all sin.*

> 1 John 1:8,9: If we claim to be without sin, we deceive ourselves and the truth is not in us. 9 If we confess our sins, he is faithful and just and will forgive us our sins and *purify us from all unrighteousness*.

> 1 John 3:3: All who have this hope in him *purify themselves, just as he is pure*.

> 1 John 3:8-10: The one who does what is sinful is of the devil, because the devil has been sinning from the beginning. The reason the Son of God appeared was to destroy the devil's work. *No one who is born of God will continue to sin*, because God's seed remains in them; they, because they have been born of God...

> 1 John 5:18: We know that anyone born of God *does not continue to sin*; the One who was born of God keeps them safe, and the evil one cannot harm them.

Some today would suggest that we are cleansed from sin only as far as God sees us, not in any real terms. But Wesley was right to note that when John wrote to his loved ones in his first epistle, he undoubtedly meant that God could purify us right here, right now. Morally pure, now. Cease to sin, now.

Impossible? Yes, humanly speaking. But the God we serve can work in us this kind of a miracle; judging from passages like those above, we should expect it.

Question: Do you believe God can make you pure and complete, now?

Prayer: Pray for complete cleansing from sin, and for the Spirit's infilling.

Day Twenty-Nine

Week Five Memory Verse: James 1:4 (see p. 62)

Today's Verse: "Yet not as I will, but as you will." (Matthew 26:39)

One night during jail ministry I invited men who wanted to receive Christ to go down to the prison floor with me—facedown before God—as low as we could possibly go before Him—to receive Him. One of the guys who prayed is now a friend, a member of my congregation and our home Bible study who was wonderfully converted that evening. I asked him later what was so special about that night. He said, "It was the prayer we said down there on the concrete. You asked us with our noses on the dirty floor to 'surrender.' I had never heard it put that way before."

He did just that. He surrendered, and soon left the detention center. He retrieved his wife and children and started discipling them as he had learned to do with his own Bible while incarcerated. His transformation is one of the greatest stories of our church.

Surrender is all about waving the proverbial white flag to the Lord and asking Him to take over. It sounds simple but it is not easy—indeed, our sinful nature fights such a humble but necessary step. But my friend Michael did it.

And his life only got harder.

Several years later his case came to trial and he received a five-year sentence. But he was not overly worried. He served out that sentence as a witness for the Lord in a very dangerous prison system, entrusted his family to our church, and prayed his way through the whole ordeal.

He is one of the holiest guys I know. But it is a good thing to remember—holiness in a man's life begins with surrender.

Question: Where is it easiest, and hardest, in your life to surrender to Jesus?

Prayer: Pray that God will help you surrender at every point of your life, especially the hardest places to give Him all.

Day Thirty

Today's Verse: "Run in such a way as to get the prize. Everyone who competes in the games goes into strict training. They do it to get a crown that will not last; but we do it to get a crown that will last forever." (1 Cor. 9:25)

At the NCAA Track and Field Championships my final year in college, I gathered with a number of athletes and coaches to watch the shot put competition. I was half-watching, half-lamenting that my career as a discus thrower was now over, when an athlete from another university looked over at me and said that one of the most prominent coaches in the nation, sitting right in front of us, had talked about me during the discus contest. I asked Tom Tellez, the great coach from Houston, what he had said. He mentioned that if I could just get rid of that little hop in the middle of my spin, I would have thrown 18-20 ft. further on that day.

"What!" I said. Tellez, *the* Tellez, thought I could have thrown a lot farther if I had better form? Well, why hadn't my coach, the famous and much respected Bob Timmons, told me?

More than a little disgusted, I asked Coach Timmons about it later. He reminded me, much to my chagrin, that over and over he had tried to change my wretched form, including that little hop, but that I had always replied, "But, Coach, that's just my *style!*" In other words, despite my coach's efforts, I had rejected correction and fallen far short of a national championship.

There is no holiness without the humility that comes with accountability. We must be open to changing our lives and have open ears and an open mind to be ready to adjust our lives at any point where the Lord chooses. If not, we fall far short of our potential in Christ.

Question: Where is your "style" in conflict with God's?

Prayer: Pray that the Lord might check your "style" on the various aspects of your life—money, sexuality, power, relationships, etc.—and help you to change it to reflect His holiness.

Day Thirty-One

Today's Verse: "He will also keep you firm to the end, so that you will be blameless on the day of our Lord Jesus Christ." (1 Corinthians 1:8)

A church was constructed in Hillsboro, Illinois in 1903; by 1987 that ecclesiastical edifice had taken on the name "Church Street Pub"—a bar and a restaurant. The stained glass windows remained, but the Sunday School room became a bar with all the normal alcoholic accoutrements. Plans were in the works to make the pulpit a stage; the pews were to be cleared out to make way for a dance floor.

Dale Lingle, owner of the pub, noted a conspicuous absence, however. Two pictures of Jesus, once featured in the sanctuary windows, were taken down and donated to a local church. Lingle observed, "Having Him in here would make me feel real uncomfortable!"

In Lloyd C. Douglas' classic *The Robe*. The character Marcellus asks Justus after Christ's ascension, "Where do you think He went?"

> "I don't know, my friend. I only know that he is alive—and I am always expecting to see Him. Sometimes I feel aware of Him, as if He were close by." Justus smiled faintly, his eyes wet with tears. "It keeps you honest," he went on. "You have no temptation to cheat anyone, or to lie to anyone, or hurt anyone—when, for all you know, Jesus is standing beside you."
> "I'm afraid I should feel very uncomfortable," remarked Marcellus, "being perpetually watched by some invisible presence."
> "Not if that presence helped you defend yourself against yourself, Marcellus. It is a great satisfaction to have someone standing by—to keep you at your best."[7]

Have Jesus around to keep us at our best? That would be a privilege, an honor, and what holiness is all about.

Question: Does Jesus ever make you uncomfortable, nervous? Why?

Prayer: Thank Him for being closer to you than you are to yourself...to keep you at your best.

Day Thirty-Two

Week Five Memory Verse: James 1:4

Today's Verse: "Devote yourselves to prayer, being watchful and thankful." (Colossians 4:2)

Perhaps one of the best places to begin a study of prayer is the familiar Lord's Prayer that Jesus taught the disciples. Here E. Stanley Jones discovered an interesting insight.[xii] Working with the pronouns of the prayer, he noticed that there seemed to be two distinct and important movements.

> *Our Father* in heaven, hallowed be *Your name, Your kingdom* come, *Your will* be done on earth as it is in heaven. *Give us* today our daily bread. *Forgive us* our debts, as we also have forgiven our debtors. And *lead us* not into temptation, but *deliver us* from the evil one.

The two sides of the prayer, as Jones sees it, are the realignment side and the result side.

REALIGNMENT	RESULT
Our Father	Give us
Your name	Forgive us
Your kingdom	Lead us
Your will	Deliver us

In the first section, we realign our lives to "Our Father": to His *name*, His *kingdom*, His *will*. In the second, we get the result: He *gives* to us, *forgives* us, *leads* us, *delivers* us. These are the alternate beats of the heart of prayer, and of holiness... *realignment-result, realignment-result.* We get as much result as we have holy realignment. This is not a magical formula but a pattern built into the universe: "The prayer of a righteous man [i.e., *rightly aligned*] is powerful and effective" (James 5:16)

Question: Why are we more enamored with the "results" side of prayer than the "realignment" side?

Prayer: Pray that God will make you a righteous and rightly aligned person of prayer.

Day Thirty-Three

Today's Verse: "...for I delight in your commands because I love them." (Psalm 119:47)

Chuck Yeager, the famed pilot, was flying an F-86 Sabre over a lake in the Sierras when he decided to buzz a friend's house near the edge of the lake. During a slow roll, he suddenly felt an aileron lock.

Says Yeager, "It was a hairy moment, flying about 150 feet off the ground upside down." A lesser pilot might have panicked, but Yeager let up on the Gs, pushed up the nose and sure enough, the aileron unlocked. Climbing to 15,000 feet, where it was safer, Yeager tried the maneuver again. Every time he rolled the problem recurred. Yeager knew that three or four pilots had died under similar circumstances, but to date investigators were puzzled as to the source of the Sabre's fatal flaw.

Yeager went to his superior with a report and the inspectors went to work. They found that a bolt on the aileron cylinder had been installed upside down. Eventually, the culprit was found in a North American plant. He was an older man on the assembly line who ignored instructions about how to insert that bolt, because he knew bolts were supposed to be placed head up, not head down. Yeager says nobody ever told the man how many pilots he killed.[xiii]

Our "instructions" are the *Holy* Bible. To ignore the instructions puts us, and others, in eternal peril. Taking the instructions seriously leads to abundant life for us, and others. Taking His holy directions seriously is what holiness is all about in our lives.

Question: Have you ever known what the "directions" (the Bible) said but didn't want to follow those instructions? Explain.

Prayer: "Lord, even when the clear instructions seem to be something counterintuitive to our worldview, help us to obey anyway."

Day Thirty-Four

Today's Verse: "For his Spirit joins with our spirit to affirm that we are God's children." (Romans 8:16/NLT)

Guy Lefrancois tells of a fun ploy by some undergraduate psychology students he once knew.[xiv] After lectures on B.F. Skinner regarding operant conditioning and behavioral shaping, the sly students attempted to corroborate the professor's words by an informal, semester-long experiment. Essentially, the lessons of the professor boiled down to this: rewarded or reinforced behavior means the greater probability of continued behavior.

So, a half-dozen students decided to become "head nodders." As a graduate-level professor, I can tell you that a head nodder is a super reinforcer to a teacher. That student echoes that yes, someone is listening and yes, they resonate with what is being said.

The head nodders, however, nodded to affirm not the content but the professor's pacing. When he quit moving, they quit nodding. After only four lectures or so, says Lefrancois, the professor paced incessantly, to the delight of the six students. That accomplished, they decided to extinguish that behavior and reinforce lecturing from one corner of the room. This too was managed easily. The next step was to condition lecturing from another corner. They successfully achieved the desired behavior modification, and the professor never knew that his classroom manner was being conditioned by the smiles and nods of just a handful of students.

The holy person stops and asks: Who and what is forming my inner life and my behavior? One thing is for sure, my inner life and hence my entire being is affected by the people, the circumstances, and the situations that I confront and how I act and react to them. At the least, holy people look to God in the midst of their responsibilities and seek His nod and affirmation for both the content and the direction of their lives.

Question: Whose "head-nodding" did you take seriously before your relationship with Jesus? In what way how has that now changed?

Prayer: Pray to look to God and God alone for approval for your life.

Day Thirty-Five

Week Five Memory Verse: James 1:4

Today's Verse: "For the LORD is the great God, the great King above all gods." (Psalm 95:3)

When people get older we frequently bemoan the fact that...well, we are getting older. But I love the people who recognize that because they are older they are now one year improved over last year, and more holy.

C.S. Lewis, in *Prince Caspian*, masterfully portrays a discussion, after a time of separation, between the Savior-figure Aslan the Lion and the child Lucy.

> "Welcome, child," he said.
> "Aslan," said Lucy, "you're bigger."
> "That is because you are older, little one," answered he.
> "Not because you are?"
> "I am not. But every year you grow, you will find me bigger."[xv]

A bigger God, not because He is, but because we can now perceive it, makes a life of holiness worth pursuing. But here is the secret, it would seem: not just getting older chronologically, but growing in our Christlikeness at the same time. Real education, I have heard, is the construction of the soul: a construction that continually strengthens and enlarges the soul and enables it to reflect the beauty of God's holiness. God, in this scenario, is the construction foreman.

Questions: What is necessary for our souls to grow? What habits of the heart can ensure such growth? Is there a new habit that might need to be utilized in your life?

Prayer: For the employment of such habits—or "means of grace"—in our lives so that we might grow daily into the holy people He wants us to be.

Day Thirty-Six

Week Six Memory Verse: 1 John 3:9 (see pg. 62)

Today's Verse: "As it is written: 'They have freely scattered their gifts to the poor; their righteousness endures forever.'" (2 Corinthians 9:9)

"Genuine holiness," says Frederick Coutts, "will find its expression in unrewarded service to the last, the least and the lost."

A Brahman from India attended a meeting where Christians glowingly described how Christ had saved them. "You people say you are saved," declared the Brahman. "So am I. As Christ has saved you, so Krishna has saved me." The missionary in charge of the meeting replied, "I am very glad to hear that you are saved—very glad indeed. Now we are going down to the outcaste quarters and are going to see what we can do for these poor people. We will sit on their beds and in their houses and will share their lives to help them. Well you join us?" The Brahman looked down and said, "Well, sahib, I am saved, but I am not saved that far."[xvi]

How saved are we? Enough to take the Gospel out of our churches and into the lives of people who desperately need our Savior?

Kublai Khan, in 1266, requested the Roman pope to "Send me 100 men skilled in your religion...and so I shall be baptized, and then all my barons and great men, and then their subjects. And so there will be more Christians here than in your parts." Two Dominicans were sent but turned back. Twelve years later, the Pope sent five others. *The Almanac of the Christian World* calls this the "greatest missed opportunity in Christian history."[xvii]

In Matthew 4:18ff. Jesus, after His temptation in the wilderness, begins His ministry in earnest by calling disciples to Himself. The very next thing that is recorded is that He took these men with Him to begin ministering to the untouchables of His culture—those with pains and diseases, those oppressed with demons, epileptics and paralytics. The Holy One in the flesh wasted no time moving towards the marginalized and continued to touch them throughout His ministry. He headed to the places of greatest need.

Questions: Is ministry to the "marginalized" a holy essential? A Christlike non-negotiable? Why? Why not?

Prayer: Pray that the Lord would lay on your heart a place of ministry to the "untouchables" of our neighborhoods.

Day Thirty-Seven

Today's Verse: "Jesus went throughout Galilee, teaching in their synagogues, proclaiming the good news of the kingdom, and healing every disease and sickness among the people." (Matthew 4:23)

In Frank Tillapaugh's important volume, *Unleashing the Church*, he contrasts the church as it has too often become—a fortress, and the church as it was meant to be—unleashed.

> The fortress church puts up its building, starts its programs and concentrates primarily within its walls. The church unleashed is not unconcerned with what goes on within its church buildings, but it is only partially focused there. In the church unleashed an individual's primary ministry may be within one of many traditional church programs such as Sunday School. But there is an equal chance that his ministry may be in a prison or working with a foreign student. In either case, the norm is people-oriented ministry.

Early in his book, Tillapaugh notes the difference between two meetings he attended: one of a parachurch organization and the other, a regional denominational gathering. The parachurch meeting was marked by excitement and anticipation. Their passion was evident as area directors reported growth in conversions, staffs, training centers, evangelistic activities. These people were clearly convinced that their world could be won for Christ. A short time later, Tillapaugh observed the denominational gathering. There, instead of, "How can we win our world for Christ?" the question was, "How can we hang on for another year?"

The Church is basically "holiness, unleashed." Too often, however, we devolve into "how can we hang on for another year?" The former is what the local church was meant to be; the latter a sad farce.

Questions: What keeps a church from unleashing? What should inspire us?

Prayer: Pray for your local church, and every person in that church, to be unleashed from a fortress mentality.

Day Thirty-Eight

Today's Verse: "Run in such a way as to get the prize. Everyone who competes in the games goes into strict training. They do it to get a crown that will not last; but we do it to get a crown that will last forever." (1 Cor. 9:25)

A.W. Tozer wrote many wonderful books, a thousand penetrating insights. But he was never more on target than when he penned these words in *The Knowledge of the Holy:* "What comes into our minds when we think about God is the most important thing about us."

> The history of mankind will probably show that no people has ever risen above its religion, and man's spiritual history will positively demonstrate that no religion has ever been greater than its idea of God....We tend by a secret law of the soul to move toward our mental image of God...Always the most revealing thing about the Church is her idea of God.[xviii]

In my morning devotions I frequently utilize the Psalms. Beside Psalm 86:15 I have penciled in the margins "Holiness."

> But you, Lord, are a compassionate and gracious God, slow to anger, abounding in love and faithfulness.

It may not be the full-orbed definition of holiness, but it is what I have nonetheless deemed "holiness in a nutshell." And the words are a quotation from God Himself:

> Then the LORD came down in the cloud and stood there with him and proclaimed his name, the LORD. And he passed in front of Moses, proclaiming, "The LORD, the LORD, the compassionate and gracious God, slow to anger, abounding in love and faithfulness..." (Exodus 34:5-6)

Wouldn't it be a beautiful thing to "move towards this mental image of God?"

Question: What is your mental image of God? What first comes to mind?

Prayer: "God of the Exodus and of the Psalms—make me compassionate and gracious, slow to anger and abounding in love and faithfulness."

Day Thirty-Nine

Week Six Memory Verse: 1 John 3:9

Today's Verse: "Therefore go and make disciples of all nations, baptizing them in the name of the Father and of the Son and of the Holy Spirit, and teaching them to obey everything I have commanded you. And surely I am with you always, to the very end of the age." (Matthew 28:19-20)

In the movie, *Superman* there is a scene where Clark Kent is upset and frustrated after a football game in which he was reduced to being a manager. He possesses supernatural powers yet must hide them from peers who don't accept him because he is not a star, only a team manager. Kent's father slips an arm around the soon-to-be "Superman" and says "Son, you are here for a special reason. I don't know what that reason is; but I know one thing, it's not to score touchdowns."

What is the special reason for the existence for humankind? Perhaps we could think of it like this: everybody, using the terms of higher education, should be considered a double major with a minor. The first major would be "Holiness." "Be holy for I am holy" says Scripture (Leviticus 11:44, et. al.) Second major: "The Great Commission" or "going to make disciples of all nations." And the minor? Your vocation—that is, what you will do occupationally through which you will "be holy" and fulfill the "Great Commission."

You occupationally want to be a lawyer? That is your minor. Holiness and the Great Commission are your majors. Ditto if you want to work in a bank. Or, be a plumber...or a doctor...or a teacher.

Let's say that you have already assumed an occupation before these new educational requirements took place. Then discover a way to either find a job that fits these "majors" or remold your present job into a profound avenue for holy living and the discipleship of the lost.

Question: How could your "minor" be more of what God wants it to be?

Prayer: "Lord, forgive me what I get my majors and minors out of whack. I want to major in holiness and the Great Commission, and use my work to further Your glory and Your kingdom."

Day Forty

Week Six Memory Verse: 1 John 3:9

Today's Verse: "And they were calling to one another: 'Holy, holy, holy is the LORD Almighty; the whole earth is full of his glory.'" (Isaiah 6:3)

People in their hearts need a sense of transcendence. If they find it in the Church and her ministries it is wonderful. But if they don't find it there, the souls of people will intuitively seek it elsewhere.

Think about the sport mentioned in yesterday's devotion—football. Hardly a mention of God at all once a game is underway. But the people gather together at their cathedral (stadium) wearing their Sunday best (team colors, jerseys). They sit together and sing worship songs (team chants) and the priests, choir and altar boys (players, coach and trainers) start their observances on the Holy of Holies (field). The offering (ball) is maneuvered to the altar (goal line and goal post) in anticipation of a sacrifice (score!). Our team is "the holy" and the opponents and their fans are "the profane," of course. Much time, money and emotional energy is spent on this week-to-week athletic drama (weekly Sunday services).[xix]

Christians might decry such a thought, but honestly, it is nothing more, really, than people trying to get in touch with something bigger than themselves, something transcendent, something...holy.

Daniel Wann [2001], a leading sport psychologist at Murray State University, says, "The similarities between sport fandom and organized religion are striking. Consider the vocabulary associated with both: faith, devotion, worship, ritual, dedication, sacrifice, commitment, spirit, prayer, suffering, festival, and celebration."

So, what is the difference between the worship on fall Friday nights, Saturday afternoons and Sunday versus the worship of God on Sunday mornings? Many things, one would hope, but none more than this: the object of our worship—Father, Son and Holy Spirit—and the objectives this God has for our lives.

Questions: Is our church as exciting and renewing as our favorite sports team? Why? Why not?

Prayer: Pray that God will help you separate "games" (of sports and other varieties) from "the holy."

Day Forty-One

Today's Verse: "Then, after desire has conceived, it gives birth to sin; and sin, when it is full-grown, gives birth to death." (James 1:15)

The late, great satirist Malcolm Muggeridge once said that "Human depravity is at once the most empirically verifiable fact yet most staunchly resisted datum by our intellectuals."[xx] The world without God desperately wants to see itself as sinless. But we all know better.

One of the ways the Bible is strong on the concept of sin is the variety of words used to describe it. The prominence of a culture's concepts are frequently recognized in the language it utilizes. Donald Metz draws upon seven Hebrew words in the Old Testament and 12 Greek terms in the New to demonstrate the variety of ways we can disappoint God.

Hebrew	Greek
Sin as "missing the mark"	Sin as transgression
Sin as crookedness/perversion	Sin as unrighteousness
Sin as rebellion	Sin as lawlessness
Sin as wickedness	Sin as unfaithfulness
Sin as unfaithfulness	Sin as debauchery
Sin as evil	Sin as perverted desire
Sin as iniquity	Sin as irreverence
	Sin as enmity
	Sin as depravity
	Sin as active evil
	Sin as a violation
	Sin as an offense

We're guilty, it would seem. Except for this: "My dear children, I write this to you so that you will not sin. But if anybody does sin, we have an advocate with the Father—Jesus Christ, the Righteous One. He is the atoning sacrifice for our sins, and not only for ours but also for the sins of the whole world." (1 John 2:1-2)

Question: Which descriptors of sin line up with your common understanding?

Pray: Thank God for Jesus' work on the cross and His grace to overcome sin.

Day Forty-Two

Today's Verse: "'Teacher, which is the greatest commandment in the Law?' Jesus replied: 'Love the Lord your God with all your heart and with all your soul and with all your mind.'" (Matthew 22:36-37)

Holiness, says Oswald Chambers, means "unsullied walking with the feet, unsullied talking with the tongue, unsullied thinking with the mind—every detail of the life under the scrutiny of God. Holiness is not only what God gives me, but what I manifest that God has given me."

Hymn writer Frances Havergal understood this when she wrote one of the greatest of her hymns: "Take My Life."

> Take my *life* and let it be consecrated, Lord, to Thee.
> Take my *moments and my days*, let them flow in endless praise.
> Take my *hands* and let them move at the impulse of Thy love.
> Take my *feet* and let them be swift and beautiful for Thee.
>
> Take my *voice* and let me sing, always, only for my King.
> Take my *lips* and let them be filled with messages from Thee.
> Take my *silver and my gold*, not a mite would I withhold.
> Take *my intellect* and use every pow'r as Thou shalt choose.
>
> Take my *will* and make it Thine, it shall be no longer mine.
> Take my *heart*, it is Thine own, it shall be Thy royal throne.
> Take my *love*, my Lord, I pour at Thy feet its treasure store.
> Take *myself* and I will be ever, only, all for Thee.

Every detail, every body part, every resource, every emotion taken captive by Christ. We offer these to Him (consecration) and He makes them beautiful for His glory (sanctification).

Question: Of Havergal's list, which is your biggest challenge today— your hands, your feet, your voice, your lips, your money, your love, etc.?

Prayer: "Lord, by Your grace, make me 'ever, only, all for Thee.'"

Day Forty-Three

Week Seven Memory Verse: Leviticus 11:45 (see p. 62)

Today's Verse: "It is God's will that you should be sanctified: that you should avoid sexual immorality." (1 Thessalonians 4:3)

Decades ago an evangelical leader I truly admired fell into sexual immorality. He admitted to an adulterous relationship that had taken place over several months. He resigned his influential position, confessed his transgression, repented of the indiscretion and was able to maintain a strong marriage with his wife.

I was floored and so was a good bit of evangelical America at the time. The downfalls of some in leadership had not been surprising. But this man shocked us with his admission.

About a month later, he was interviewed in *Christianity Today.* He described, briefly, how the affair had come about, asked forgiveness, and then reported why he felt the need to confess publicly and resign his presidency. *CT* quoted him in this revealing passage:

> Satan's ability to distort the heart and the mind is beyond belief. I assume the responsibility for what I did; I made those decisions out of a distorted heart.
>
> In addition, I now realize I was lacking in mutual accountability through personal relationships. We need friendships where one man regularly looks another man in the eye and ask questions about our moral life, our lust, our ambitions, our ego.[xxi]

Holiness demands many things, not the least of which are these: first, recognizing that there is a devil and that he is a distorter. And, second, rigorous, mutual accountability with a few trusted friends.

Question: Mutual accountability is lacking in many Christian relationships. Why?

Prayer: Pray that God would show you fresh ways to be accountable to someone else or, perhaps, a small group of believers.

Day Forty-Four

Week Seven Memory Verse: Leviticus 11:45

Today's Verse: "Religion that God our Father accepts as pure and faultless is this: to look after orphans and widows in their distress and to keep oneself from being polluted by the world." (James 1:27)

In 1947, Robert Pierce's work for *Youth for Christ* took him to China. There, he met a lady named Tena Hoelkedoer who dropped an abandoned child in his lap and asked "What are you going to do about her?" Pierce gave Hoelkedoer the last bill in his pocket and agreed to send five dollars each month to help care for the child. He would later write these words in the flyleaf of his Bible: "Let my heart be broken with the things that break the heart of God."

When Jesus said, "Blessed are those who mourn" he undoubtedly meant that our hearts should break over things that break His heart. But who wants to spend their lives crying? Jesus might answer, "Holy people." John Wesley put it this way for the Christians he was trying to disciple:

> Let us be employed, not in the highest, but in the meanest, and not in the easiest but the hottest, service—ease and plenty we leave to those that want them. Let us go on in toil, in weariness, in painfulness, in cold or hunger, so we may but testify the gospel of the grace of God. (Acts 20:24) The rich, the honourable, the great, we are thoroughly willing (if it be the will of our Lord) to leave to you. Only let us alone with the poor, the vulgar, the base, the outcasts of men. Take also to yourselves 'the saints of the world': but suffer us 'to call sinners to repentance"; even the most vile, the most ignorant, the most abandoned, the most fierce and savage of whom we can hear. To these we will go forth in the name of our Lord, desiring nothing, receiving nothing of any man (save the bread we eat while we are under his roof), and let it be seen whether God has sent us.[xxii]

Question: We should love "the poor, the vulgar, the base, the outcasts of men." Why is this so hard for many of us?

Prayer: "Lord, help our hearts to be broken over the things that break your heart."

Day Forty-Five

Week Seven Memory Verse: Leviticus 11:45

Today's Verse: "...because the Lord disciplines the one he loves, and he chastens everyone he accepts as his son." (Hebrews 12:6)

Holiness means that man is pliable in the hands of God. And it means that God shapes. But this shaping might involve pressing and pulling and pinching and molding us into His image. It may bring pain.

> When God wants to drill a man,
> and thrill a man and skill a man.
> When God wants to mold a man
> to play the noblest part
> When He yearns with all His heart
> to create so great and bold a man
> That all the world might be amazed
> Watch His methods, watch His ways.
>
> How He ruthlessly perfects,
> whom He royally elects
> How He hammers and hurts him
> And with mighty blows converts him
> Into trial shapes of clay
> While his tortured heart is crying
> And he lifts beseeching hands
>
> How He bends, but never breaks
> When this good He undertakes
> How He uses whom He chooses
> And with every purpose fuses him
> And with mighty acts induces him
> To try His splendor out.
> God knows what He is about.
> (unknown author)

The holy person is willing to undergo ruthlessness, hammering, hurt and tears to be made usable and purpose-filled for God's glory.

Question: What kind of hard shaping is God doing in your life right now?

Prayer: Pray that God will accomplish His shaping and molding of your life, no matter how hard.

Day Forty-Six

Week Seven Memory Verse: Leviticus 11:45

Today's Verse: "The way of a fool seems right to him, but a wise man listens to advice." (Proverbs 12:15)

The Wesleyan band meetings included the following practices to establish people in a life of holy living:

Any of the following questions may be asked as often as occasion offers; the four following at every meeting.

> 1. What known sins have you committed since our last meeting?
> 2. What temptations have you met with?
> 3. How were you delivered?
> 4. What have you thought, said, or done, of which you doubt whether it be sin or not?

Eleven other questions were given for use, these among them:

- Do you desire to be told of your faults?
- Do you desire to be told of all your faults, and that plain and home? Do you desire that every one of us should tell you, from time to time, whatsoever is in his heart concerning you?
- Consider! Do you desire we should tell you whatsoever we think, whatsoever we fear, whatsoever we hear, concerning you?
- Do you desire that, in doing this, we should come as close as possible, that we should cut to the quick, and search your heart to the bottom?
- Is it your desire and design to be on this, and all other occasions, entirely open, so as to speak everything that is in your heart without exception, without disguise, and without reserve?

Most Christians today would rather people just mind their own business than do such probing. But Wesley knew it was hard to cultivate Christlikeness without regular, holy interrogation.

Question: Which of the above questions are the most intimidating? Why?

Prayer: Pray that you could find someone in your life willing to ask the tough questions for spiritual gain.

Day Forty-Seven

Week Seven Memory Verse: Leviticus 11:45

Today's Verse: "So Solomon did evil in the eyes of the LORD; he did not follow the LORD completely, as David his father had done." (1 Kings 11: 6)

The Hebrew word for profane is *chalal* (kha LAL) and it means basically what you would think it means—vulgar, defiled, polluted, dishonored. But there is another meaning—"common."

To profane the name of the Lord is to make His name like all the other gods'—of no noble character, wooed by superstition, manipulated with magic. And, actually, that seems to be what usually happens in the Old Testament.

Leviticus flat lays down some tough law concerning a god named Molech:

> The LORD said to Moses, "Say to the Israelites: 'Any Israelite or any alien living in Israel who gives any of his children to Molech must be **put to death**. The people of the community are to **stone him**. I will set my face against that man and I will **cut him off from his people**; for by giving his children to Molech, he has defiled my sanctuary and <u>profaned</u> my holy name. If the people of the community close their eyes when that man gives one of his children to Molech and they fail to put him to death, I will **set my face against that man and his family and will cut off** from their people both him and all who follow him in prostituting themselves to Molech. (Leviticus 20:1-5)

Wouldn't happen to you, me or us? Well, it apparently happened to what might arguably be the smartest guy of his day, or any day. 1 Kings 11 is one of the most pitiable chapters in the Bible for it tells of what the wealthiest, most blessed, most divinely discerning man, became. In the fourth chapter of 1 Kings it is reported that Solomon received from God wisdom and insight and understanding—well beyond any peer. He spoke 3,000 proverbs and wrote over a thousand songs. People from far and wide came to hear the king's wisdom. My bet is that he had Leviticus and surrounding books memorized.

But seven chapters later in the story come these chilling phrases:

> He followed Ashtoreth the goddess of the Sidonians, and Molech the detestable god of the Ammonites. So Solomon did evil in the eyes of the LORD; he did not follow the LORD completely, as David his father had done. On a hill east of Jerusalem, Solomon built a high place for Chemosh the detestable god of Moab, and for Molech the detestable god of the Ammonites. (1 Kings 11:5-7)

Profane! And yet do we also make God's name *common* when those of us who go by the designation "Christian" spend more time and attention on our college football team than we do His causes or His Body? Or when we spend our money almost precisely the way our unchurched friends spend theirs? Or when our favorite Christian chants go something like this:

> "The only difference between sinner and saint
> is one is forgiven and the other ain't."

The ONLY difference? Ouch.

About Molech—most scholars say that the cult of this god sacrificed children by throwing them into a fire to guarantee his favor. Alternatively, other researchers have suggested that children were given up by their parents to be trained as temple prostitutes.

Wisest man in the world? Yoked to Molech and others, Solomon died a disappointment to God. As could be expected, the Chosen People followed his example and became unholy as Molech and the other gods were unholy: profane, common.

Question: What should be the biggest differences, if God has His way in our lives, between sinners and saints?

Prayer: "Holy Spirit, there is a fire I want my family to know. YOUR fire. The fire of the Spirit. They will not be the wisest people of their generation, in all likelihood, but let them KNOW You and love You with ALL their hearts, souls, minds and strength. Amen."

Day Forty-Eight

Week Seven Memory Verse: Leviticus 11:45

Today's Verse: "You will seek me and find me when you seek me with all your heart." (Jeremiah 29:13)

To go "all the way" is what God wants for us. After salvation, we should all be encouraged to seek what has frequently been called "entire sanctification." Very often, the believer must walk with Jesus a while to see the depth of his sin. Whether that length of time is some weeks, or months, or years, there should come a point in the believer's life when he desires a deeper relationship with Jesus.

There are many ways to describe the experience of this "all the way-ness" or this "entire" kind of holy reality. Frank Thompson lists some of these terminologies from Scripture[xxiii]:

Baptism with the Holy Spirit	Heart purity
The filling of the Spirit	The baptism with the Holy
Entire sanctification	Ghost and with fire
Death of the self-life	The circumcision of the heart
Pure love	Perfection
Living in the Spirit	The fullness of the Spirit
Walking in the Spirit	The fullness of God
Overcoming power	Full salvation
Entire consecration	The higher life
Holiness	The deeper life
Perfect love	The gift of the Spirit
Christian perfection	The gift of the Holy Spirit
The life of faith	The Holy Spirit poured out
The rest of faith	The sealing with the Holy Spirit
Sanctification	The wisdom from above
A clean heart	

Question: Which of these terminologies do you typically associate with giving your all to Christ and thus knowing His sanctification?

Prayer: "Lord, I want to be know these words in reality. Show me what I must do to receive your gift of sanctifying grace."

Day Forty-Nine

Week Seven Memory Verse: Leviticus 11:45

Today's Verse: "For God did not appoint us to suffer wrath but to receive salvation through our Lord Jesus Christ." (1 Thessalonians 5:9)

There are many ways to lead people to Christ. One model is not only a good outline to keep in mind for evangelism but in experiencing for yourself entire sanctification and leading others to do the same.

First, for the evangelism outline. The method uses SCAT – S-C-A-T.

> Recognize: You are a **S**inner.
> **C**hange.
> **A**sk
> **T**rust.

That we are **sinners** is a universally understood truth. The Bible teaches that "all have sinned and fall short of the glory of God. (Romans 3:23) Jesus asked us to **change** when he challenged us with these words and others like them: "Repent (change!) for the kingdom of heaven has come near. (Matthew 4:17) We need to **ask** Jesus into our lives. "Everyone who calls on the name of the Lord will be saved." (Romans 10:13) And then a new believer must **trust** that God has done what He said He would do:

- If you confess with your mouth that Jesus is Lord and believe in your heart that God raised him from the dead, you will be saved. (Romans 10:9)

- Anyone who believes in Jesus will not be disappointed. (Romans 10:11)

- If anyone acknowledges that Jesus is the Son of God, God lives in him and he lives in God. (1 John 4:15) *All verses here from the NLT.*

Questions: How were you led to the Lord? Which of the "SCAT" points were the most challenging for you to believe?

Prayer: Ask the Lord for someone in your life that doesn't yet know Him with whom to share this SCAT outline.

Day Fifty

Today's Verse: "Consecrate yourselves and be holy, because I am the Lord your God." (Leviticus 20:7)

The "SCAT" acronym also works well for those wanting to enter into a deeper experience with the Lord and consecrate all their lives to Him so He can make all of their lives beautiful for Him.

Along the "SCAT" outline, take seriously these four steps:

> Thank God for **S**aving you
> **C**onsecrate (dedicate to God) *ALL* your life to Him. All that you
> think, all that you feel, all that you choose, all your behavior, all
> that you own.
> **A**sk Him to make holy (sanctify) what you have given Him.
> **T**rust that He has done exactly that—sanctified you wholly and that
> He has given you the purity and the power to live exactly as He
> wants you to live.

A friend of mine[xxiv] frequently precedes this outline with the following challenge for audiences: "There is going to come a time when you recognize that Jesus is calling you to a deeper walk with Him and desires to cleanse you from everything that is not Him. You will want more. And some of you are there today—you just want more. Well, there is more. Jesus through His Holy Spirit wants to purify you and empower you to live on another level of love for Him and for others. If you sense God is calling you to this kind of deeper life, come down here and meet us at this altar..."

He has rarely said such a thing without significant numbers of people coming forward to consecrate their "everything" to the Lord.

The appeal above contains these words: He "*desires to cleanse you from everything that is not Him.*" Another way to put it is we have to utterly die. A friend talks about having his funeral one day at the side of a road. Under conviction from the Lord he stopped his vehicle, got out of his car and cried out to God as his desires, his hopes, his plans, his possessions were put on the altar and he died completely to them. It was his "funeral," he says. Only then could the Holy Spirit have His way in him.

Once someone gives their all and God has sanctified into this beautiful life of "more" what needs to happen then?

- They should *testify* to the Body of Christ and others of their experience of going deeper with God and the fact that they are now purified and empowered to live for Him as never before.

- They should seek Him with renewed fervor through the *"means of grace"*—Bible study and memorization, prayer, fasting, devotional reading—both personally and with a mentor who can lead and guide to deeper levels of spirituality.

- They should *serve.* This means sharing the gospel with the unchurched, serving the poor and finding ways to help the local church function well according to their spiritual gifts. Sacrificial service is one of the most underrated "means of grace" necessary for continued entire sanctification, but absolutely critical for maintaining the experience.

God wants to expand His kingdom through all believers but He does His best work through those who are wholly given to Him. God will show the way forward and change the world through those who are *entire.*

Henry Varley, a British preacher who had befriended the young D.L. Moody in Dublin, once told Moody words that changed his life. "The world has yet to see what God can do with a man fully consecrated to him," said Varley.

"By God's help," said Moody, "I aim to be that man."

Much Kingdom fruit came from Moody's life and many others through Christian history who dared by God's grace to consecrate all so that God might entirely sanctify that all.

Question: What part of "all" is God asking you to consecrate right now?

Prayer: Pray for grace to give "all," that He might make that "all" beautiful.

Memory Verses

Scripture memory is a powerful discipleship tool. Dallas Willard, professor and author:

> Bible memorization is absolutely fundamental to spiritual formation. If I had to choose between all the disciplines of the spiritual life, I would choose Bible memorization, because it is a fundamental way of filling our minds with what it needs. This book of the law shall not depart out of your mouth. That's where you need it! How does it get in your mouth? Memorization.[xxv]

Memory work can be done either individually or in a group. Since this devotional might be in a daily group, here are some tips:

- The leader should initially read a small portion of the passage and then, as the portion is read again, participants should try to say the verse with the leader. In unison! As best you can! Indeed, sometimes you must mumble along!

- Start with one sentence. Add another sentence the next day. Repeat two or three times. Add one on each subsequent day.

- After the passage is memorized thoroughly (along with the verse number) repeat all that has been memorized each setting before new memory work is begun.

- Meals are a good opportunity for memory work (particularly if you eat together at least daily). If not, choose another time (perhaps before tucking the kids into bed?) where this devotional guide and discussion, prayer and memory work can be accomplished.

- When these verses have been memorized, keep going. Memorizing the rest of your life will revitalize your Christian walk.

Memory should accomplish the following, and much more!

- Strengthen your mind for God.
- Increasingly give you the mind of Christ.
- Give you holy words to meditate on whenever you have a few moments of quiet.
- Give you a great foundation for communication with God.
- Give you confidence in your daily walk and boldness for your next challenge.

The Weekly
Memory Verses

Week One: As obedient children, do not be conformed to the passions of your former ignorance, but as he who called you is holy, you also be holy in all your conduct, since it is written, "You shall be holy, for I am holy." (*1 Peter 1:14-15*)

Week Two: Make every effort to live in peace with everyone and to be holy; without holiness no one will see the Lord. (*Hebrews 12:14*)

Week Three: Jesus replied: "'Love the Lord your God with all your heart and with all your soul and with all your mind.'" (*Matthew 22:37*)

Week Four: Jesus replied, "I tell you the truth, everyone who sins is a slave to sin. Now a slave has no permanent place in the family, but a son belongs to it forever. So if the Son sets you free, you will be free indeed." (*John 8:34-36*)

Week Five: Perseverance must finish its work so that you may be mature and complete, not lacking anything. (*James 1:4*)

Week Six: No one who is born of God will continue to sin, because God's seed remains in him; he cannot go on sinning, because he has been born of God. (*1 John 3:9*)

Week Seven: "I am the LORD, who brought you up out of Egypt to be your God; therefore be holy, because I am holy." (*Leviticus 11:45*)

Endnotes

[i] Richard S. Taylor, ed., *Beacon Dictionary of Theology* (Kansas City: Nazarene Publishing House, 1984) "Holiness," by Dennis Kinlaw, 259. Much of this is from Kinlaw's article.

[ii] Ibid.

[iii] Ibid.

[iv] "Remembering David Wilkerson", *The Corner: A National Review Blog*, April 28, 2011

[v] Allan Coppedge, *Portraits of God: A Biblical Theology of Holiness* (Downers Grove, Ill.: Intervarsity Press, 2001), 32. The Personal Revealer categories were adjusted a bit for this author's personal preference.

[vi] *Christian Century*, November 5, 1980, 1058-1062

[vii] John N. Oswalt, *Called to Be Holy: A Biblical Perspective* (Nappanee, Ind.: Evangel Publishing House, 1999), 1.

[viii] Ibid, 2.

[ix] Samuel Miller, *The Dilemma of Modern Belief* (New York: Harper & Row), 80-81.

[x] Author's files.

[xi] C.S. Lewis, *The Screwtape Letters* (New York: MacMillan Publishing Company/Collier Books, 1961), 39.

[xii] E. Stanley Jones, *The Way* (Garden City, N.Y.: Doubleday and Company, 1978), 216

[xiii] Chuck Yeager, *Yeager* (New York: Bantam, 1985), 185.

[xiv] Guy LeFrancois, *Psychology for Teaching, Fifth Edition* (Belmont, California: Wadsworth Publishing Company, 1985), 49.

[xv] C.S. Lewis, *Prince Caspian: Book 2 in the Chronicles of Narnia* (New York: Macmillan Publishing Company, 1951), 136.

[xvi] E. Stanley Jones, *Christ of the Round Table* (London: Hodder and Stoughton, 1928), 96.

[xvii] Edythe Draper, ed., *The Almanac of the Christian World* (Wheaton, Ill.: Tyndale House Publishers, 1990), 310.

[xviii] A. W. Tozer, *The Knowledge of the Holy* (New York: Harper & Row Publishers, 1961), 9.

[xix] Simon Ponsonby, *The Pursuit of the Holy* (Colorado Springs, Co.: David C. Cook, 2010), 20.

[xx] Muggeridge, quoted in Ponsonby, 71.

[xxi] "A Talk with the McDonalds," *Christianity Today*, July 10, 1987, 38.

xxii John Wesley, "A Farther Appeal to Men of Reason and Religion, Part III" Works [BE], 11, 315-316.

xxiii W. Ralph Thompson, *The Road to Heaven: The Way of Holiness* (Indianapolis, In.: Light and Life Press), 38-39.

xxiv Crawford Howe, former district superintendent of the Church of the Nazarene.

xxv Dallas Willard, "Spiritual Formation in Christ for the Whole Life and Whole Person" in *Vocatio*, Vol. 12, no. 2, Spring, 2001, 7.

41545025R10040